P

RED LILIES AND FRIGHTENED BIRDS

M.L. THANGAPPA (b. 1934) was born in Kurumpalapperi, Tirunelveli district, Tamilnadu. Educated at St John's College, Palayamkottai, he taught Tamil for over twenty-five years in the various colleges of the Puducherry government until his retirement in 1994. He served on the editorial board of the Tamil monthly *Thenmoli* (1962–67). An accomplished poet, his books in Tamil include *Adichuvadukal, Uyirppin Athirvukal, Ethu Valkai?* and *Nunmaiyai Nokki*. His translations from Tamil literature into English range from Sangam poetry and didactic poetry to the songs of St Ramalingam, Subramania Bharati, and Bharatidasan. He has won the Bharatidasan Award (1991) of the Government of Tamilnadu, and the Sirpi Literary Award (2007) for lifetime achievement in poetry. Active in the Tamil language rights movement, he is also a founding member of the Puducherry Ecological Society. His translations from the Tamil classics have appeared in Penguin as *Love Stands Alone: Selections from Tamil Sangam Poetry*. Thangappa lives with his family in Puducherry.

A.R. VENKATACHALAPATHY (b. 1967) studied in Chennai and took his PhD in history from the Jawaharlal Nehru University, New Delhi. Now professor at the Madras Institute of Development Studies, Chennai, Chalapathy has taught at universities in Tirunelveli, Chennai and Chicago, and has held research assignments at Paris, Cambridge and Harvard. He has published widely on the social, cultural, and intellectual history of colonial Tamilnadu, both in Tamil and in English. His publications include *In Those Days There Was No Coffee: Writings in Cultural History, The Province of the Book: Scholars, Scribes, and Scribblers in Colonial Tamilandu*, a translation of Sundara Ramaswamy's *J.J.: Some Jottings*, as well as the edited volumes *Chennai, Not Madras*, and *In the Tracks of the Mahatma: The Making of a Documentary*. He has also edited M.L. Thangappa's *Love Stands Alone: Selections from Tamil Sangam Poetry*.

Red Lilies and Frightened Birds

Muttollayiram

Translated from the Tamil by
M.L. Thangappa

Edited and introduced by
A.R. Venkatachalapathy

PENGUIN BOOKS

PENGUIN BOOKS
Published by the Penguin Group
Penguin Books India Pvt. Ltd, 11 Community Centre, Panchsheel Park,
New Delhi 110 017, India
Penguin Group (USA) Inc., 375 Hudson Street, New York, New York 10014,
USA
Penguin Group (Canada), 90 Eglinton Avenue East, Suite 700, Toronto,
Ontario, M4P 2Y3, Canada (a division of Pearson Penguin Canada Inc.)
Penguin Books Ltd, 80 Strand, London WC2R 0RL, England
Penguin Ireland, 25 St. Stephen's Green, Dublin 2, Ireland (a division of
Penguin Books Ltd)
Penguin Group (Australia), 250 Camberwell Road, Camberwell, Victoria
3124, Australia (a division of Pearson Australia Group Pty Ltd)
Penguin Group (NZ), 67 Apollo Drive, Rosedale, Auckland 0632,
New Zealand (a division of Pearson New Zealand Ltd)
Penguin Group (South Africa) (Pty) Ltd, 24 Sturdee Avenue, Rosebank,
Johannesburg 2196, South Africa

Penguin Books Ltd, Registered Offices: 80 Strand, London WC2R 0RL,
England

First published by Penguin Books India 2011

Translation copyright © M.L. Thangappa 2011
Introduction copyright © A.R. Venkatachalapathy 2011

Cover photograph by V.K. Rajamani, taken from *The Mucukunda Murals in
the Tyāgarājasvāmi Temple, Tiruvārūr* by V.K. Rajamani and David Shulman,
published by Prakriti Foundation, Chennai 2011

10 9 8 7 6 5 4 3 2 1

ISBN 9780143064855

Typeset in Sabon by Eleven Arts, Delhi
Printed at Chaman Offset Printers, Delhi

for
Visalakshi Thangappa
and
Anitha Chalapathy

The land of Kothai,
deft wielder of a deadly spear
with poison-tipped, leaf-shaped head,
knows no turmoil
except that
caused by the water birds.
For when the red lilies
bloom in the waterlogged fields,
the birds panic,
thinking the water is on fire.
They fly helter-skelter,
trying to guard their nestlings
under their wings.

CONTENTS

INTRODUCTION
Of Spears and Bangles

That Tamil is a classical language is now a commonplace in the scholarly world. However, its living and unbroken literary tradition of over two millennia remains unrecognized to a large extent. Widely anthologized and translated, *Tirukkural* and Sangam poetry have come to stand for the entire corpus of classical Tamil poetry and didactic wisdom. In truth, the Tamil poetic tradition has much more to offer. With its brilliance and variety *Muttollayiram* presents an ideal text from which to launch further poetic forays into the landscape of Tamil poetic imagination.

Literally, *Muttollayiram* could mean either 'three nine-hundreds (of poems)' or 'nine hundred (poems) on the three (monarchs)'. Unfortunately, given the fact that only some 130 of them survive, the numbers themselves are a subject of another debate, and even the meaning of the ambiguous title has evoked considerable controversy. For a long time it was thought that *Muttollayiram* consisted of 2,700 poems with 900 on each monarch—an erroneous view that some hold on to even now. However, even by the standards of Tamil's bad luck where a large corpus of writings has been wiped out by calamities such as tsunamis, bigotry, and apathy, it is somewhat far-fetched that only about a hundred out of 2,700 should survive. The confusion about the actual numbers was ultimately cleared by

S. Vaiyapuri Pillai, the enormously erudite if controversial scholar, who cited two grammatical texts, *Ilakkana Vilakka Pattiyal* and *Prabandha Deepikai*, which refer to a genre called 'Thollayiram' that consists of 900 poems.

Therefore, it is now clear that *Muttollayiram* consists of 900 poems in all, with 300 each devoted to a monarch hailing from one of the three Tamil dynasties—Cheras, Cholas and Pandyas. The bulk of them (108 plus an invocatory poem) come from a fifteenth-century anthology of *puram* poems, *Purathirattu*; quotations from medieval commentaries account for the rest. Poems from *Muttollayiram* have been cited or quoted in a variety of pre-colonial commentaries of mostly grammatical texts, indicating its continued importance in Tamil literary culture. It is evident that *Muttollayiram* is not an anthology but a unified work by a single author who, however, is anonymous, with neither written record nor even oral tradition to throw a single shaft of light upon his identity. Like all Tamil literary texts, the dating of *Muttollayiram* is a subject of debate. Based on internal and external evidence, S. Vaiyapuri Pillai dated it to the early part of the ninth century CE while T.V. Sadasiva Pandarathar dated it to the sixth century. As we shall see below the earlier date is more plausible.

It was not until 1905 that these poems were first culled from *Purathirattu* by Ra. Raghavaiyangar and published separately. The credit for drawing attention to the exquisite poetic qualities of *Muttollayiram* and celebrating it should go to T.K. Chidambaranatha Mudaliar (1881–1954), the renowned connoisseur of poetry. Since then, despite their meagre quantity, these poems have captured the hearts of the cognoscenti and been frequently reprinted and glossed. *Muttollayiram* has also been translated at least twice into

English—P.N. Appuswami (1977) and A.V. Subramanian (1984); into Sanskrit—A.V. Subramanian (1993); and into Hindi—S. Subramanian (1996). There is also a German study of the text by Ulrike Niklas (1987).[1]

***

Why should this book of hundred-odd poems, admittedly incomplete, capture the fancy of Tamil readers and warrant a new English translation? Readers familiar with Sangam poetry will easily recognize the setting and the themes of *Muttollayiram*. The conventions of *akam* and *puram* mingle almost seamlessly, extending the elaboration of Sangam themes to their limits.[2]

Coming centuries after the flowering of Sangam poetry, the earliest corpus of Tamil literature, *Muttollayiram* nevertheless presents many continuities. The Chera, Chola and Pandya kings, who are even mentioned in the second and thirteenth rock edicts of Ashoka (third century BCE), and still somewhat nascent in the Sangam age, emerge in *Muttollayiram* as full monarchs in all their glory. A number of terms for rulers—such as *irai, ko, kilavan, velir, kurisil, kottram, mannan, arasu*, and *ventar*—occur in the more ancient corpus dated to the cusp of the Common Era. The usage of these terms, the Marxist Tamil scholar K. Sivathamby observes, is often marked by considerable flexibility; but this flexibility 'is seen only in the case of those who go high up in the ladder of the authoritative position'.[3] Despite plausible arguments that

---

[1] See Manikandan (ed.), *Muttollayiram* for a complete bibliography.

[2] For an introduction to Sangam poetry see Venkatachalapathy, 'Introduction: Tradition, Talent, Translation' in Thangappa, *Love Stands Alone*.

[3] Sivathamby, *Studies in Ancient Tamil Society*, p. 40.

'there is nothing, whether in literature, epigraphy or archaeology, which points to the institution of the state in that society',[4] it is, however, evident that the *ventar* are clearly distinguished from the lesser kings/chieftains; referring to monarchs, this term is used exclusively in relation to these kings. 'With *ventu/ventar* we come to the most powerful and militaristic personality of the rulers to emerge in Tamilnadu.'[5] As K. Kailasapathy states, the term *mu ventar* was 'exclusively and collectively used by the bards of the [Sangam] Anthology poems for these three kings. Hence the term has come to have a specific meaning of "crowned heads".' He adds that this phrase 'has a rich literary usage behind it'.[6] Further, as Sivathamby says, the 'tradition of referring to the other two [monarchs] when eulogizing the third' is also very common.[7]

The three royal lineages of antiquity—Chera, Chola and Pandya—are extolled in 138 poems of *Purananuru*, the Sangam anthology of four hundred *puram* poems. *Muttollayiram* refers to them by a variety of titles (some probably dating from their pre-monarchic past): the Pandya is called 'Makadumkone', 'Maran', 'Koodal Koman', 'Thennan', 'Cheliyan' and 'Valudi'; the Chola is referred to as 'Valavan', 'Sembian' and 'Killi'; and the Chera is addressed as 'Kothai', 'Vanchi Ko', 'Mandhai Ko' and 'Vanavan'. On the other hand, the teeming scores of valorous and proud chieftains and local tribal chiefs in Sangam poetry—praised in as many as 141 *Purananuru* poems (and thus outnumbering the panegyrics on the monarchs)—appear only

---

[4] Veluthat, 'Into the "Medieval" and Out of It: Early South India in Transition', p. 10.

[5] Sivathamby, *Studies in Ancient Tamil Society*, p. 46.

[6] Kailasapathy, *Tamil Heroic Poetry*, pp. 86–87.

[7] Sivathamby, *Studies in Ancient Tamil Society*, p. 48.

as enemies to be routed or as vassals heaping tributes at the monarchs' feet. The tragic story of Pari, the munificent chieftain of the Parambu mountain country, who is treacherously defeated by the joint action of the three monarchs in a protracted siege and is the hero of many a *Purananuru* poem, would be out of place in *Muttollayiram*.

Further, it is very interesting to note that the three monarchs are not mentioned in *Muttollayiram* by name at all but identified by their dynasty and related titles. A unified conception of the Tamil country ruled by three traditional dynasties animates the text. Even in *Purananuru*, we have references to Tamilakam (the Tamil country) which the monarchs aspire to bring under their rule. The continual feuds among the monarchs notwithstanding, a unified conception of the three kingdoms constituting a single Tamil country was present at least in the minds of poets. The celebrated *Silappadhikaram* takes the name of each of its three cantos from the capitals of the *muventar*: Pukar, Madurai and Vanchi. It would appear that *Muttollayiram* is following this tradition by having odes to the three monarchs in a single work. Further, we also have two surviving instances where the Chola and Pandya kings are referred to as *Tamilar/Tamilnar peruman* (lord of the Tamil people).

Of each monarch, the glory of his country and city, the military adventures of his horses and elephants, his prowess in war, the exploits of his weapons and the ruining of the enemy country—themes familiar from *Purananuru*—are elaborated by *Muttollayiram* in great poetic detail and hyperbole. The royal insignia, listed as befitting the 'sceptred monarchs' in *Tholkappiyam*, the great 2000-year-old Tamil grammatical treatise, in its chapter on poetic conventions—'army, flag, parasol, drum, horse, elephant, chariot, garland, crown'—find adequate mention in these poems.

But over three-quarters of the *Muttollayiram* poems speak of how nubile women, deeply infatuated, pine and long for the king. Bangles slip from wrists become thin with lovesickness, while the skin develops patches in lovesick pallor—the consummation taking place only in dreams rather than in reality as the women yearn for the king marching past on his elephant or horse in ceremonial procession. The prudish mother and foster mother who do their best, but in vain, to stop the heroine from indulging in her love, and the helpful go-between, her friend—the familiar dramatis personae from *akam* poetry—figure here very prominently. As a majority of the poems may be classified as Kaikkilai, the theme of one-sided and unrequited love, it is not surprising that they are all in the voice of the lovelorn girl. There are also some poems in the words of the mother/foster mother. Perhaps not a single theme would be unfamiliar to a reader of Sangam poetry.

In a little-noticed essay, K. Sivathamby argues that political authority in early Tamilnadu was 'inchoate' and goes on to assert that 'a highly personalized monarchy had arisen in [early] Tamilnadu'.[8] A fascinating chapter in Kesavan Veluthat's study of the political structure of early medieval south India analyses what he calls 'the self-image' of this 'personalized' monarch:

> Several aspects went into the making of this image—origin myths, dynastic traditions, genealogies, etc. through which the dynasty in general sought legitimation as well as

---

[8] Ibid., p. 54.

through the presentation of an individual king as having acquired ksatriya status, as a *chakravartin*, as a warrior-hero, as a protector and fountain-head of all dharma, as a munificent donor, as a divine figure, as an attractive mien, and finally as a patron of arts and culture.

Going into the origins of these constitutive elements of the fashioning of this self-image, Veluthat adds:

While most of these aspects were inspired by stereotypes presented in Sanskrit literature, there were aspects which had an equally local, Tamil bearing which took into account traditions of the Sangam literature concerning dynastic connections and also myths about individual ancestors and culture centres.[9]

A reading of *Muttollayiram* suggests that while many of these aspects do indeed cohere with Veluthat's depiction of the 'self-image' some aspects critically do not. Firstly, the origin myths 'drawing typically' from the '*itihasa–purana* tradition of northern India' are not evident in *Muttollayiram* and therefore it cannot be said to have 'participated in a pan-Indian tradition of the origin of dynasties'.[10] Nor does it claim typical Kshatriya status for the monarchs, 'a major component of the image of royalty'.[11]

How then is one to reconcile the 'self-image' delineated by Veluthat with the representation of the monarch in *Muttollayiram*?

---

[9] Veluthat, *Political Structure of Early Medieval South India*, p. 30.
[10] Ibid., p. 34.
[11] Ibid., p. 45.

Despite the fact that he claims to draw his evidence from 'contemporary royalist literature in the main, preserved in the copious *prasastis* and other forms of court literature, both in Sanskrit and Tamil', it is apparent from the references that Veluthat has cited that the data comes overwhelmingly, if not exclusively, from inscriptions and not court literature. Further, he is primarily concerned with the period from after the seventh century. If we accept T.V. Sadasiva Pandarathar's dating, then *Muttollayiram* would have to be assigned to the sixth century or about a century earlier than the historical moment discussed by Veluthat.

***

What accounts for *Muttollayiram*'s continuing fascination?

Firstly, *Muttollayiram* is written in the *venba* metre, a quatrain verse form with three lines of four feet each and a last line of three feet with a formulaic ending. A demanding prosodic form, *venba* has been likened to dancing with manacles on. The author of *Muttollayiram* is a crafty wielder of the *venba*, about as masterful as the monarchs who wield the spear in his masterpiece. This would certainly mean much to a native reader of the poetry, but is impossible to reproduce in translation. (Y. Manikandan has argued that the *venba* used in *Muttollayiram* is still evolving and therefore suggests this as another ground for assigning an early date to the text.)

This formalistic justification apart, the genius of *Muttollayiram* lies in fusing *akam* and *puram* conventions in an original—in both senses of the term, of being the first and being new—way. *Tholkappiyam*, the paradigmatic Tamil grammatical treatise that codifies not only *eluthu* (letter—phonetics) and *chol* (word—morphology and syntax) but also *porul* (content—poetics or rhetoric), is particularly strict in defining and segregating the two complementary and overarching categories of *akam* and *puram*. *Akam*, the inner, is all about love and conjugality. And *puram*, the outer, is concerned with everything in the world except *akam*. *Akam* conventions are in turn strictly defined. Any reference to an actual person or even an identifying allusion would render a poem—*akam* in every other respect—a *puram* one. And of love too, only the five classical love situations are acknowledged as worthy of *akam* status. These are Kurinji (which tells of clandestine meetings of the lovers set in the hills); Mullai (narrating the hopeful waiting of the wife in the pastoral region); Marutam (of the infidelity of the man and the sulking of his wife, set in the plains); Neidal (of the wife's anxious anticipation for the husband's return in the littoral tracts); and Palai (of the lover's departure and travel in search of wealth, education or adventure, set in the wilderness). On the other hand, Kaikkilai, one-sided or unrequited love, and Perumthinai, mismatched love or excessive lust, fall in the *puram* category.

By the definition of *Tholkappiyam*, all the love poems of *Muttollayiram* would fall only in the Kaikkilai category, thus accounting for their inclusion in *Purathirattu*, the anthology of *puram* poems. But this is not the Sangam age—though we are not sure how many centuries later it is. However, *Muttollayiram* is unique in giving a rounded picture of secular figures, the monarchs, portraying not only their martial prowess but also their amorous exploits. The representation of the *mu ventar*, the three monarchs, in *Muttollayiram* has lingered long and imprinted itself in the Tamil psyche.

Thus *Muttollayiram* marks a new phase in Tamil literary tradition, bridging, as it were, Sangam and post-Sangam poetic traditions. If Sangam poetry is a corpus with its own cosmology where one poem makes *full* sense only in relation to the entire body of writings, *Muttollayiram* handles many Sangam *akam* and *puram* themes with abandon and flourish without too many of these restrictions and constraints. Similarly, if Sangam poetry is marked by a certain sparseness of diction, *Muttollayiram* explores Sangam themes intensively and extends them to the full, indulging in controlled exaggeration and understated hyperbole. While *Muttollayiram*, like Sangam poetry, uses a few fixed epithets and noun epithets, usually for prosodic reasons, its genius lies in the almost infinite improvisations it makes in set themes.

> Enemies,
> throw open the doors
> of your castles!
> Set free your elephants and horses
> from their trappings of war!
> For today,
> the day of Uthiradam,
> our southern lord,
> great charioteer,
> celebrates his birthday,
> and he will not fight today.

Here in *Muttollayiram* 7, we find the poet offering a reprieve to the enemies on the day of the Pandya king's birth star.

If *Purananuru* 20 talks of the Chera king, Mantharancheral Irumporai, who is the protector of all his subjects:

People who live under your canopy
know no other fire
than the fire of the burning sun
and the fire of the cooking stove.
They know no other bow
than the rainbow.
And no other weapon than the plough.
Putting down your powerful foes
you have consumed their soil,
but your own soil
is never consumed by anyone else
except pregnant women
who have morning sickness.
Your fort stands against arrows.
Your sceptre stands for righteousness.
In spite of new ill-omens coming
and old ill-omens going
your land is the safest haven for your people.
You are such a noble ruler,
the whole world fears for your safety.[12]

Muttollayiram extends it to the inanimate:

The land of Kothai,
deft wielder of a deadly spear,
with poison-tipped, leaf-shaped head,
knows no turmoil
except that

---

[12] Thangappa, *Love Stands Alone*, pp. 124–25.

caused by the water birds.
For when the red lilies
bloom in the waterlogged fields,
the birds panic,
thinking the water is on fire.
They fly helter-skelter,
trying to guard their nestlings
under their wings.

If Sangam poetry has very little to say about the prowess of the war horses and elephants, *Muttollayiram* is most elaborate in its description of their exploits.

Charging like demons,
the horses of Maran
flew at the enemy elephants,
snapping their collar bands,
which upset the seated kings
who fell to the ground.
The horses stepped on them,
kicking off their crowns of gold,
and trampling on their golden necklaces.
And soon their hooves
glistened with gold
like a goldsmith's touchstone.

If *Muttollayiram*'s handling of *puram* themes is brilliant, *akam* themes shine even better. The boundless flair for improvisation that these poems seem capable of—vividly invoking the travails of the lovelorn women who pine for the monarch on ceremonial procession—is staggering.

> Dear friend,
> with slender arms
> full of bangles
> and eyes like swords,
> let me ask you
> one thing about my mother
> who forbids me
> to look at Maran—
> who has conquered
> many a land,
> who wields
> flaming battle-hungry spears
> and who wears garlands of
> fresh-blown flowers—
> had she never been young?

A more effective denunciation of the prudish mother who tries to prevent the heroine from looking at the king would be hard to conceive, or so one would think, but poem 117 probably outdoes this:

> Look at the doors in this street!
> All have worn-out hinges.
> For mothers keep shutting them
> and daughters keep throwing them open.
> This happens

> whenever the prince Kothai,
> wearing fresh flower garlands
> and riding a sturdy horse,
> passes along the street
> and love-mad girls
> rush to have a glimpse of him.

It is such prolific creativity in the variations of themes, one better than the other, that is the hallmark of *Muttollayiram*. In tribute, perhaps, later poets have taken them up—as, for instance, *Kalingathupparani* does in playing on the idea of worn-out hinges. In fact, a distinct genre, the Ula, emerges in the early part of the second millennium where the poem itself is structured around the ceremonial procession of the monarch, and the deity. Thus *Muttollayiram* also presages some later-day genres.

***

Ultimately poems, whether original or translated, have to stand by themselves without the crutches of introductions and glosses. M.L. Thangappa is ideally suited to the task as he is a consummate interpreter and translator of Tamil poetry into English.

Born in Kurumpalapperi, a small village in Tirunelveli district—not far from the mythical birthplace of Tamil, the Pothikai hills—Thangappa comes from a family of Tamil pandits. Thangappa's father and at least two of his uncles were Tamil teachers. A somewhat precocious child, he could recite scores of Tamil poems when barely a boy. (This immersion in Tamil verse at an impressionable age has had a very peculiar effect on his prosodic skills. His keen ear can always detect minor variations or improvisations in metric forms even when not being able to actually name them.) When Thangappa went to the then venerable St John's College, Palayamkottai, his grasp of idiomatic English, already imbibed from reading English fiction, was further buttressed by reading the Bible and the Romantic poets, taught by learned teachers including European clergymen who lectured there. As a Tamil teacher for over twenty-five years, lecturing at various colleges of the Puducherry government, classical Tamil literature has been the staple of his teaching, parsing and interpreting the terse poems for generations of students.

The range of his translations is staggering. From Sangam literature to Bharati and Bharatidasan, Thangappa has translated a considerable body of Tamil literary texts into English over the last five decades. Ever the perfectionist, he always maintains that his translations are incomplete—something that explains why many of them have not yet found their way into print. His belief that selections rather than full translations are better recommended has not particularly helped in remedying this situation. This is probably the first time that he has translated a full text—which also speaks for the brilliance of *Muttollayiram*. Despite his vast reading Thangappa is no pedant, preferring to rely on intuition rather than scholarship. If his ear for English is astonishing, his grasp of Tamil is almost incredible. Unlike many translators—both renowned and not so renowned—who rely on commentaries, old and new, to get to a text, Thangappa reads classical Tamil like one would the morning newspaper.

* * *

Given *Muttollayiram*'s history of recovery into print, as outlined above, a note on the edition used for this translation is in order. *Purathirattu*, from which *Muttollayiram* is drawn, is grouped under various *puram* themes—a scheme followed by the first editor of *Muttollayiram*, Ra. Raghavaiyangar (originally published as an appendix to the literary monthly *Sentamil*, vol. 3, no. 3, 1905, with 105 poems; later reprinted separately as a book by Madurai Tamil Sangam in 1935 with the addition of another three poems recovered from a newly discovered palm-leaf manuscript). S. Vaiyapuri Pillai's 1938 edition of *Purathirattu* for the Madras University press, still the best, provides 110 poems, including one poem in a highly mutilated form cited in the editorial introduction. T.K. Chidambaranatha Mudaliar's edition (1943), intended for the connoisseur, follows its own scheme, given its editor's quirks.

I discovered that Thangappa, as is his wont, relied often on memory rather than follow a printed text. My task, apart from providing notes and prodding Thangappa, has been to compare the translation with Na. Sethuragunathan's edition (1946, reprinted 1952, 1958) and suggest revisions. Sethuragunathan's was the first edition to classify the poems under the rubrics of the three monarchs, a convention subsequently followed by many editors. This volume includes, apart from the 110 poems, twenty poems culled from various commentaries, though these have been contested by many scholars.[13] Apart from these editions there are also a number of bazaar editions. Y. Manikandan's edition, forthcoming from the Central Institute of Classical Tamil, is based on all extant manuscripts and printed editions; with his erudite introduction and definitive readings of the

---

[13] In particular, these include poems 58, 59, 60, 61, 63, 64, 68, 69, 70, 75, 78, 79, 80, 81, 83, 84, 104, 105, 106 and 107.

poems, Manikandan's edition promises to become the standard displacing all other editions.

Select Bibliography

Chidambaranatha Mudaliar, T.K. (commentary). *Muttollayiram*. (Chennai: Thiruvarasu Puthaka Nilaiyam, 2004; first edition 1943).

Kailasapathy, K. *Tamil Heroic Poetry*. (Oxford: Clarendon Press, 1968).

Manikandan, Y. (ed.). *Muttollayiram*. (forthcoming).

Sadasiva Pandarathar, T.V. *Tamil Ilakkiya Varalaru: AD 250–AD 600*. (Annamalai Nagar: Annamalai University, 1963).

Sethuragunathan, Na. (commentary). *Muttollayiram*. (Tirunelveli: Saiva Siddhanta Works Publishing Society, 1958; first edition 1946).

Sivathamby, K. *Studies in Ancient Tamil Society*. (Madras: New Century Book House, 1998).

Thangappa, M.L. *Love Stands Alone: Selections from Tamil Sangam Poetry*. (New Delhi: Penguin Viking, 2010).

Vaiyapuri Pillai, S. (ed.). *Purathirattu*. (Chennai: University of Madras, 1938).

Vaiyapuri Pillai, S. *Ilakkiya Chinthanaikal* (volume one of collected works of S. Vaiyapuri Pillai). (Chennai: Vaiyapuri Pillai Ninaivu Mandram, 1989).

Veluthat, Kesavan. *The Political Structure of Early Medieval South India*. (New Delhi: Orient Longman, 1993).

Veluthat, Kesavan. 'Into the "Medieval" and Out of It: Early South India in Transition', Presidential address, Medieval Indian History Section, Indian History Congress, XLVII Session, Bangalore, 1997.

Venkatachalapathy, A.R., 'Introduction: Tradition, Talent, Translation' in Thangappa, *Love Stands Alone: Selections from Tamil Sangam Poetry*. (New Delhi: Penguin Viking, 2010).

A NOTE ON THE MONARCHS

The Pandya kings ruled the southernmost part of the Tamil country, covering the composite districts of Madurai, Tirunelveli, Kanyakumari and Ramanathapuram of modern Tamilnadu; hence the repeated references in *Muttollayiram* to the Pandya kings as 'the lords of the South'. Their capital city was Madurai on the banks of the Vaigai. The earliest references to them are found in the second and thirteenth rock edicts of Ashoka (third century BCE). Legend and literary tradition associate the Pandya kings with the Tamil language and literature; and they are said to have patronized the three Sangams, or Tamil academies, where poets congregated to debate and authorize literary works. Similarly, the Pothikai hills, the legendary birthplace of the Tamil language, are also associated with them. The Pandya kings controlled the port of Korkai, famed for the richness of pearls and conch shells used to make jewellery. Their totem flower was the neem, and their royal emblem, the fish.

The early Pandya kings ruled between the third century BCE and third century CE. Thirty-seven poems in the *Purananuru*, belonging to the Sangam anthologies, extol the glories of twelve Pandya kings. The most important kings of this dynasty are Vadimbalamba Nindra Pandyan, Mudukudumi Peruvaludi and Neduncheliyan. For three centuries between the third and sixth centuries they lost power to the Kalabhras, and the dynasty was revived only in the early seventh century. The political fortunes of the Pandyas in the subsequent centuries were uneven and suffered much at the hands of the later-day Cholas. In CE 1310 Madurai was overrun by the Khiljis under the commandership of Malik Kafur.

Muttollayiram refers to the Pandya king as Tamilnarperuman, Thennan, Thennavan, Thennavarkoman, Thennanilanko, Maran, Maran Valudi, Makkadunkon, Cheliyan, Koodalkoman, Maduraiyarkoman, Thenkorkaikoman, Pothiyilkoman. His horse is referred to as *kanavattam*.

The Cholas ruled the central part of the Tamil country irrigated by the fertile Kaveri and covering the composite districts of Thiruchirapalli, Thanjavur and South Arcot of modern Tamilnadu. The Kaveri, referred to by a variety of names, is closely identified with the Cholas. The earlier references to them are found in the second and thirteenth rock edicts of Ashoka (third century BCE). The Cholas had two capitals: Uraiyur was the main capital; the other, Kaverippumpattinam or Poompuhar, was an important trading port. Thanjavur became the Chola capital only from the late ninth century. The lack of any references to Thanjavur is an important piece of evidence to assign an early date to *Muttollayiram*. Important early Chola kings include Karikalan, Nedunkilli, Nalankilli and Kopperuncholan. As many as seventy-four poems in the *Purananuru* sing the praise of thirteen Chola kings. Their royal emblem and standard was the tiger, and their tutelary flower, the *aathi* (mountain ebony).

Like the Pandyas and Cheras, the Cholas were overrun by the Kalabhras between the fourth and sixth centuries. From the ninth until the thirteenth centuries the later-day Cholas (sometimes called 'the imperial Cholas') held sway over the entire peninsula and even extended their empire beyond the seas to south and south-east Asia. Their rule was marked by the construction of massive temples across the region.

The Cholas are referred to by a variety of traditional titles in *Muttollayiram*: Killi, Valavan, Sembian, Urandaiyarkon, Puharperuman, Kaverinadan. The Chola kings' horse is referred to as *padalam*.

The Cheras are traditionally associated with the region of the present-day state of Kerala and the western regions of the Tamil country including the composite districts of Salem, Coimbatore and Nilgiris of modern Tamilnadu. In the second and thirteenth rock edicts of Ashoka (third century BCE) the Chera kings are referred to as Keralaputra (a literal translation of Cheraman or *Cheral* + *makan*). The Chera kings are the most praised in Sangam literature: *Pathittrupattu* (the Ten Decads, the first and last being lost) and twenty-seven poems in the *Purananuru* sing the glories of Chera kings. Their capital was Vanchi; its location, still a matter of debate, was probably present-day Karur. The other Chera capital, Manthai, remains unidentified. Important Chera ports were Thondi and Musiri. Celebrated Chera kings of the Sangam age are Udiyancheral, Imayavaramban and Senkuttuvan; the last is credited with bringing a stone from the Himalayas to fashion an image of Kannagi, the Tamil ideal of chastity. The Chera emblem was the bow, and their tutelary flower, the palmyra.

Muttollayiram refers to the Cheras by a variety of traditional titles and epithets such as Kothai, Vanavan, Pooliyan, Musiriyarkoman, Cherankothai, Kokothai, Vanchikoman, Manthaiko and Makkadunko.

1

He is the Primordial One
who created the sun,
the moon and the stars
which are everlasting.
How is it that people
living on this sea-girt earth
have given him a name
and call him
'Aathiraiyan'
repeatedly?

THE PANDYA PRINCE

His Glory

2

In the wars he wages
Maran, who wields a shining spear,
is sure of a glorious victory.
And the songs I sing of him
in my sweet Tamil tongue
are like the *kadamba* flowers
offered in daily worship
to the brave and powerful lord
who rides a peacock.

3

The flowers offered
by the brave Arjuna
to Krishna
were found, they say,
at the feet of Siva,
who rides a white bull.
In the same manner
flowers worn by kings
on their heads
are found at the feet
of Maran,
wearer of thickly woven garlands.

4

You had it on your chest
when you killed the demon horse,
when you performed the pot-dance,
and when you became Kovalan
to marry Punthodi.
Where have you hidden
that dark mole on your chest,
O lord of the south,
famed charioteer
and king of Koodal?

5

Pure gold adorns
Maran's land.
Works of literature,
music and dance
adorn his city.
Conches and pearls
adorn his waters.
Elephants adorn
his foothills.
And the torsos of enemy kings adorn
the sharp edge of his combat spear.

6

They say the five-headed cobra
that possesses a rare gem
lies hiding,
fearing the thunderbolt.
So too, the enemy kings of Maran,
of battle-winning arms
and bloodshot eyes,
scared of his deadly spear,
keep seeing it
in their dreams.

7

Enemies,
throw open the doors
of your castles!
Set free your elephants and horses
from their trappings of war!
For today,
the day of Uthiradam,
our southern lord,
great charioteer,
celebrates his birthday,
and he will not fight today.

His Country

8

The tiny eggs of the conch,
little round buds of the laurel tree
and the flower-pods
of the areca-nut palm
lie scattered everywhere—
they look and glisten like pearls
in the land of Thennan
whose canopy, too,
is set with shining pearls.

His City

9

Women, sulking at their husbands,
wipe off their shoulders
moist sandal paste
mixed with *kumkumam*
and throw it on the street,
turning the lanes of the city
slippery,
making people
skid and fall.

Tributes He Received

10

Do you know why
the celestial ones
do not tread on earth
while walking?
It is by order of
the southern prince
who bears the whole earth
on his shoulders
and shelters his people
under his canopy.

11

When the white canopy of Maran,
of the blue-lily garland
shaped like the full moon,
was mounted on his elephant
and taken on a parade,
the vassal kings
came rushing to him
with their tributes,
complaining,
'Is it kind of you,
great king,
to frighten us like this?'

Capturing the Enemy's Fort

12

King Maran is offended
and ready for war.
His shining spears
are battle-fit.
His war drums
start thundering.
The truant vassal kings
feel terror,
like snakes at the crash of thunder,
and flee behind the hills
where antelopes roam,
and burn with the fear
that gnaws at their stomachs.

His War Horses

13

Charging like demons,
the horses of Maran
flew at the enemy elephants,
snapping their collar bands,
which upset the seated kings
who fell to the ground.
The horses stepped on them,
kicking off their crowns of gold
and trampling on their golden necklaces.
And soon their hooves
glistened with gold
like a goldsmith's touchstone.

His War Elephants

14

The stylus: his tusk.
The palm-leaf scroll:
the broad chests of enemy kings
with spears burning with valour.
This war elephant
of our spear-wielding Maran
writes this document declaring:
'The whole world is ours.'

15

The Pandya king
wears a beautiful garland
and rides an elephant
who, too, looks beautiful
with his long, pointed tusks.
Do you know what the two tusks
do in battle?
One ploughs into the chests of enemies
and the other
breaks open their fortresses.

16

Huge as a hill,
he trumpets
like the roaring sea.
His musth
streams down
like a summer tempest.
He is swift as the wind.
Even the god of death
borrows from him
a trick or two
in the art of killing.
Such is the elephant
of Maran, the Pandya king
who wields a shining spear.

17

The war elephants
of the southern king—
whose spears emit fire—
are ashamed of
appearing before their females,
looking ugly
with tusks broken.
Attacking enemy fortresses
had given them that ugliness.
So they come covering their tusks
with the canopies of enemy kings.

His Battlefield

18

Pierced to death by spears,
the soldiers lie in the battlefield.
Their eyebrows are still
knitted in anger,
scaring away
the carcass-hunting jackals.
They stand at a distance,
howling for company.

19

Unable to bear the sight
of women from the enemy side
immolating themselves,
the king Valudi
pulled his shawl across his face
and hid his eyes.
Likewise, his elephants too
closed their eyes,
unable to bear the sight
of cow elephants from the other side
mourning their dead males.

Ruining Enemy Lands

20

These are the ruins
of mansions where once
a king, wearing laurels of victory,
held his happy court.
But now
spirits haunt the place
and barn owls
howl their eerie songs.
This is the lot of kings
who fail to submit
to the authority
of Thennan.

21

First, the cattle would be taken,
then womenfolk captured,
and lastly, all the men routed.
The whole country would be devastated
to become the haunt of spirits.
This is the fate of the lands
of the hostile princes
who refused to pay tribute
to the Pandya king
who rides a killer elephant—
a terror to the passers-by
who are warned off
by drum beats.

His Conquests

22

Formidable
even in death,
the soldiers lay there
propped up on a dead elephant,
biting their lower lips,
spears held firmly
in position,
refusing still
to give up their land.
And the victorious Pandya king,
holding his flag aloft
and wearing wreaths round his head,
stood looking at them
and felt defeated.

23

The wives of the enemies
who have provoked great Maran
of the shining garlands
have no chance of pardon
unless they come
with their clinging children,
fall prostrate at his feet
and beg for their kingdoms.
This is the cure
for his bloodshot eyes.

His Infatuates Complain

24

Thennan, southern prince,
mounting his proud elephant,
appeared in my dream
and made love to me—
which was but an illusion.
But taking it to be real,
on waking up
I felt for him
in my bed
with my tender *kanthal* fingers,
and found in it
none but my poor self.

25

Happy water-lilies,
dark blue like the clouds!
Is it because
they stood in water
and did their penance
day and night
that they are worn
by Valudi—
whose horses are swift,
whose garlands are bright and fresh
attracting the honeybees?

26

Who knows?
Some day I might
succeed in love
and walk on the heads
of these prudes
who have shut me up,
and reach into the arms
of the ruler of Madurai—
where waters
come in waves
and lap against
the sides of the storeyed mansions.

27

The bangles I wear
are of conch shells from his seas.
And my necklaces
are made of pearls from his seashells.
The sandal paste
applied on my body
comes from the Pothikai hills
of the valiant Maran.
Yet, my arms
are getting thin.

28

If I drop my bashfulness
and look at him
my modesty will be lost.
But if I do not look at him
my bangles will slip off my wrists.
I see no way
to get rid of my suffering
by feasting my eyes
on Valudi, master horseman,
whose fresh flower garland
relieves the suffering
of the honeybees.

29

Of what use
are my full, rounded breasts,
sleek and sweet
like tender palmyra nuts,
if they are not able to
plough into the cool sandal paste
on the breast of Thennan
whose elephants
have pointed tusks?

30

If I get into these waters,
splash them about
and enjoy bathing in them,
I know folk would scold me.
And if I don't,
they'd say I had
hidden my feelings.
Alas, my spear-eyed friend,
either way, the cool waters
of the river Vaigai of Maran
who rides a killer elephant
are quite a bother to me.

31

'If I am to meet my prince,
the king of Koodal
and idol of his people,
and enjoy his caresses,
let me play the game of *koodal*—
draw a circle on the sand
and see whether
both ends meet.'
Saying this she was about
to draw the circle
but withdrew her finger quickly.
'What would happen to me
if the ends do not meet?'
she said to herself.

32

Friend,
please do not tell him
about me—
my name
or my village.
Also, do not tell him
who my mother is.
Just tell the lord of the Tamils
with his hot-tempered elephant:
'There is a girl;
ever since she saw you
she has no sleep.'

33

Dear friend,
with slender arms
full of bangles
and eyes like swords,
let me ask you
one thing about my mother
who forbids me
to look at Maran—
who has conquered
many a land,
who wields
flaming battle-hungry spears
and who wears garlands of
fresh-blown flowers—
had she never been young?

34

How I crave to sing
of his flag,
his chariot,
his crown,
his necklace of pearls!

And to pound rice
in the mortar,
uttering with every stroke of the pestle
the name of Maran
who wears a garland of cool flowers.

But alas, I cannot do this;
for my mother is watching me
night and day.

35

Enamoured of the prince
of the city of Koodal,
surrounded by lush coconut palms,
my heart went in search
of his caresses.
Not knowing this
my poor mother
keeps watch
over my physical body
like a hunter
guarding an empty cage
after the bird has flown away.

36

Let them lose their kingdoms—
the arrogant princes
who refused to submit to Thennan,
who rides a spirited elephant,
and offended him,
calling him a callow youth.
Serves them right.
But why should I lose
the tender mango-leaf colour
of my complexion,
I who worshipped
his broad, handsome chest?

37

Oh, what has become of my eyes?
They mistake
dream for reality
and stare at his image
shamelessly.
But when he appears
in person,
they fight shy
of looking at him.
If this is so, my friend,
how am I going to win
the love of Maran?

38

O my foster mother,
bringing me
fresh flower garlands,
I will not uncover my eyes
even if you take my life.
For the heartless Maran,
deft wielder of swords,
who had got away with my bangles,
returned last night
and with his enormous elephant
strode into my eyes.

39

At last
I had some sleep.
But the next moment
Maran, the great swordsman,
appeared in my dream
and gripped my hand.
Believing it to be real
I shook off my sleep
and got up.
But alas,
luckless me,
I have lost
even my dream!

40

A pearl oyster,
tired after giving birth to a pearl,
crawls to the top of a dune
and awaits wistfully
the arrival of the right wave
to plunge back into the seas.
Likewise
my lovelorn soul
tarries at the palace door,
awaiting word
from the Korkai king.

41

He is the prince
of the Pothikai hills
where the hill folk
cook their rice
over a sandalwood fire.
Pining for his love
I have lost my bangles.
Go and tell him,
O winter wind,
it is quite unbecoming of him
to harass me like this
while his canopy and sceptre
proclaim his benevolent rule.

42

My poor heart
that went after the prince of Koodal
now stands at his palace door,
giving way to those who enter
and to those who come out,
and hiding itself from those who scoff.
It's like a deer
wounded with an arrow,
standing on a sandbank
and biding its time
to escape into the forest.

43

Like illness
harassing the sick
with increased vehemence
on their birthdays,
this violent winter wind
harasses me with yet greater violence
on these gloomy lovelorn evenings
passed languishing for Maran Valudi
who rides an elephant with tinkling bells.

44

I love
the warrior prince Maran,
a terror to his enemies.
I speak a thousand things about him
when he is not around.
But if I see him in person,
would I be able to
fly into his arms
and ask for his garland?
O, this bashful modesty
has been with me all my life!

45

Poor night!
It is torn between
two sets of women:
those who have
had the joy of embracing
the broad chest
of Maran
and the others who haven't.
The former say,
'Please, night,
do not go away soon,'
and the latter say,
'Go away, night!
Let dawn arrive fast.'

46

The luminous pearls
that come from oysters
are not found
in the port of Korkai alone.
They are also found
in the eyes of maidens
who long
for the embrace
of the broad, sandal-paste-smeared chest
of Maran,
whose spear is ever moist
with blood.

47

Feigning anger,
I sulked.
He tried to make peace,
but I was obstinate.
He became angry
and turned his back to me.
Then I tried to pacify him
but he wouldn't come round.
It was thus, my friend,
that the whole night passed
without my embracing
Valudi's broad chest,
cool with sandal paste
and fresh flower garlands.

48

They say that
blood is thicker than water.
I find it true, my friend.
For these bangles of mine
made of conch shells
stop slipping off my wrists
the moment they hear
the sound of the conch shell trumpet
of the king of the Vaigai land.

49

How shall I thank
the carpenter
who made this keyhole?
He has given me the chance
of peeping at the prince Makadunkone
riding past our house,
when the house itself is shut
and locked from the outside
by my prudish mother.

50

Cow elephant—
with *thudi*-like feet,
shield-like ears,
a dangling trunk
and hanging lower lip—
I beg of you:
when you enter our hamlet,
carrying on your back
the ruddy-complexioned prince
wearing sweet-smelling garlands,
please walk
close to my window.

51

Cow elephant
of Maran the prince,
I doubt
your femininity.
For when the prince
and ruler of Koodal,
whose battle-spear
reeks of raw flesh,
comes riding on you
along our street
you do not care to walk
with gentle steps.

52

O horse,
you may charge swiftly
on the battlefield,
but when you enter our village,
please have the tact
not to trot in such haste
but to walk gently,
so that,
standing behind the door,
I may feast my eyes
on the broad chest
of the prince Maran,
of sharp spears and rutting elephants.

53

How I crave
to dance and play
with this dust,
to smear it on my head,
to mix it with water
and paint patterns with it
on my bosom—
the dust raised by the hooves
of the royal horse Kanavattam
of Valudi of the golden chariot,
wearing a garland of the choicest flowers.

54

Like a lighted lamp
kept under a bushel,
the love of women
for prince Valudi,
who wears a garland of lovely flowers,
remained hidden within their hearts.
But when the prince
set out on his procession
their love couldn't be hidden.
It was all over the village,
blazing like a forest fire
at twilight.

55

When Maran
passed along our street
I stood worshipping him.
But he robbed me
of the healthy glow
of my arms.
Himself being the ruler
of Korkai of the dark sea
with roaring waves
who protects his subjects,
to whom shall I make a complaint
about his cruelty?

56

The king is bound
to protect his subjects.
And if I am
his subject,
how does it become Chelian,
with his sceptre
of unfailing justice,
to treat me cruelly
while he protects others?
It is like giving water to some
and milk to others.

57

He is the sole protector of people—
the prince Maran who wears a garland
of fresh flowers.
And he reigns over earth and heaven.
But I am a humble person—
a poor girl.
If he doesn't show me mercy,
who is there to question him?

58

Three of us girls
stood in a meandering street in Madurai,
city of many mansions,
watching the royal procession.
One girl admired
the golden hood of the elephant.
The other admired
the elephant's beauty.
Happy girls!
They were innocent.
Only I, destined to suffer,
admired the lovely garland
worn by Thennan,
mounted on the elephant's back
and holding his shining leaf-shaped spear.

59

The cruel king—
wearing a garland
of nectar-filled flowers—
who took away
the healthy bloom of this girl,
is no mere ruler of Vanchi.
He is the great monarch
and protector
of all the five Tamil states.
Belonging to the tradition
of good governance
he doesn't swerve
from the path of righteousness.

60

A calf forages
the *ulundu* crop
and runs away,
while an innocent donkey
grazing nearby
gets his ears cut
as punishment.
Likewise,
it is my eyes
that feasted on Valudi
but it is my arms
that have become pale.

61

My poor heart!
Could it have
reached the palace by now,
or perhaps be returning from there?
Or is it still waiting at the gate,
arms akimbo,
for the opportune hour
to meet the prince?
I know not.
Only, it went after
the prince Maran,
whose yard is full of
trumpeting elephants
and whose garlands
swarm with bees.

THE CHOLA PRINCE

His Glory

62

The Mantara mountain
as its handle and shaft,
the heaven
its cloth,
the moon
its round central piece,
the canopy of the
Chola prince,
ever victorious in war,
shelters the whole earth
surrounded by the seas.

63

You had it on you
when you broke
the *kurunda* tree—
the dark mole on your chest.
O king—
in whose land of rivers
the gulls do not roost on the trees
but fall asleep on the haystacks—
where have you hidden it now?

64

The king of the land of rivers
and the god of the basil garland
are different
in their actions.
The earth which the king
won with his victories
the god obtained
by begging.

His Country

65

In the land of Kokilli,
who rides a beautiful elephant,
the farm workers on guard
climb on hayricks
and call out loudly
to their cohorts—
like Death
mounted on a killer elephant,
making his battle call.

His City

66

The heart
of Valavan's beautiful city of
Urandai,
strewn with an assortment of flowers
discarded as waste
the previous evening
by flower sellers,
looks in the morning
like the sky
sporting a rainbow.

Tributes He Received

67

Stop for a while, O kings,
bring your tributes later.
For yesterday too
there was a crowd of kings
who paid their obeisance.
Their crowned heads grazing
them in large numbers,
the feet of our king,
ruler of Urandai,
are badly bruised.

His War Horses

68

Valavan the great,
king of a water-rich land,
where the floodgates
are plugged with
the straw from harvested paddy,
has hands
that give generously
like the rain clouds.
And his battle horse
is swift as the wind.
He charges at the enemy kings,
knocks down their crowns of gold
and tramples on their necklaces.
His hooves,
glistening with their gold,
look like touchstones.

His War Elephants

69

In the sky
the full moon wanes,
fearing the war elephant
of the king Killi
who bears the earth
on his shoulders.
Witnessing the elephant
trample the white canopies
of enemy kings,
his anger unabated,
the moon is terrified
that, crossing the skies,
the angry beast
might turn on her.

70

When the war elephant of Killi—
who is bounteous like the rain clouds,
wears battle-anklets
and wields an unfailing spear—
sets out
with his powerful trunk
and hanging lower lip,
that which snaps
is not the chain which binds him,
but the *thalis*
of the wives of his enemies.

71

Breaking through the railings
and storming the inner fort
of the powerful enemy king,
the elephant of Killi
the hot-tempered,
lifts upon his tusks
the huge door of the fort
and stands,
resembling a ship set sail
on the cold sea.

72

Tusks broken
while tearing down
enemy fortresses,
toenails worn out
knocking down the crowns
of enemy kings,
the elephants of Killi
returned from the battlefield,
worn out and war weary.
Ashamed to present themselves
before their females
in such bad shape
they lingered
outside the gates.

73

Putting one foot
on Kanchi,
another on Ujjain
of the surging waters,
and another
on the land of Eelam,
the elephant of Killi,
the king of Koli,
storms his way
with colossal strides.

74

Here comes
the war elephant
of our spear-wielding Killi,
trailed by
hovering vultures and kites,
followed by jackals
rushing from every side,
and accompanied by
female ghouls
wearing beautiful garlands
and dancing wildly.

His Battlefields

75

Shattered skulls
blown-out brains
mangled bodies
broken bones
disembowelled intestines
floating in a river of blood
and ghouls dancing—
this is the battlefield
where the triumphant Killi
routed the Karnatakas.

76

Skulls of crowned kings,
the containers;
scattered brain-matter,
the oil poured;
and the intestines,
the wicks.
Thus the graveyard ghouls
light the lamps of death
and, holding them aloft,
dance with joy
on the battlefield
in which the prince Sembian
crushed his enemies.

Ruining Enemy Lands

77

Among the womenfolk
fleeing their land
were those pregnant
who gave birth to children
in the woods.
The infants were laid
on quilts of dry leaves.
The call of the barn owl
became their lullaby.
This was the plight of the people
in the towns of the kings
who did not praise
the name of Sembian.

His Conquests

78

The spear of the ruler
of the fertile Ponni land,
held aloft in peace,
was the moon.
The mercy granted
to the repentant kings
was the sweet moonlight
shed on them.
The thousand pairs of palms
brought together in tribute
were the lotuses
that closed their petals
at the moon's appearance.

79

That which was conquered
with the power of arms,
that which was covered with
multifarious glory,
that which is borne
by the Chola king
on his strong shoulders,
that which is ruled justly
by the wheel of law
is the earth
which Thirumal
pressed down with just one foot.

80

Behold the angry war elephants
of the Chola king
whose beautiful Kaveri land
lacks no water
even when the heavens fail.
No sooner were their ankles
fitted with battle-bands
than the lotus feet of the enemy kings
fastened with fetters.

His Munificence

81

After looking at the face of Chenni—
the ruler of Urandai,
the great warrior
who wields the spear that never fails—
the pleading eyes of mendicants
will never again look at the face of another
to beg for wealth.

82

The priests get their gifts
of cows and gold.
The poets ride away
on elephants large as the Mantara hill.
Thus are people happy
on the day of Revathi,
the birth star of Killi,
wielder of a shining spear.
Only the spiders
lose their webs.

83

How much wealth has the king Chenni
who wields a shining spear?
No one can tell.
While wealth
keeps flowing in from one side
from his conquests
it also keeps flowing out
on the other
by way of charity.
No one knows
how much.

84

King Chenni
sliced up flesh from his own body
and weighed it on a scale
to save the life of a fugitive pigeon.
Is this gallantry for being generous?
Or courage in enduring physical pain?
Neither.
It is his noble character.

His Infatuates Complain

85

Throw the doors open first!
Let us think of the damage later.
For greater will be the harm
if these girls started dying.
So let them be free
to feast their eyes
on the Chola prince,
ruler of Urandai
and leader of the Tamils,
who wears a garland
of cool *athi* flowers.

86

Cow elephant,
carrying on your back
Valavan who wears
a garland of blue lilies,
you walk
immodestly fast.
You don't have the
feminine grace
of the women of this land—
where the dark clouds
hovering on the woods
look like clusters
of blue lilies.

87

To the joy of the city's maidens
the Chola prince,
wielder of shining spears,
mounted his royal horse Padalam
and rode in state.
Feminine eyes,
gleaming and rolling
at every window,
resembled the *kayal* fish
wriggling and rolling
in a fisherman's net of blue.

88

It was my kohl-lined eyes that looked.
It was my heart that went after him.
But alas, my innocent arms
are being punished.
Is this the justice
meted out by Uraiyur Valavan
while he passes in state
along the city streets?

89

A ruler should take,
by way of taxes,
only one-sixth
the income.
But how is it,
my broad-hipped friend,
that the ruler of this land of rivers
has taken away
more than that?
He has my heart,
my modesty
and the bloom of my maidenhood.

90

When he appears in my dream
my eyes remain closed.
And when he comes in person
coyness prevents me
from looking at him.
My eyes and my coyness
have both given a bad name
to the justice of the king of Puhar,
who owns a fleet of ships
that crisscross the swirling seas.

91

Killi,
munificent giver
who tosses away
elephants as gifts
and who wears a garland
of cool fresh flowers,
appeared in my dream and
made away with my clothes.
Is this the nature of his royal justice?
I shall expose him
in front of his retinue
when I meet him in the street.

92

They say
the young prince Valavan,
who wears a garland of
fresh-blown lilies,
is the protector of the earth.
If so,
how is it then
he failed to protect me
from the heartless cruelty
of the cowherd's flute?

93

They say
Killi—
who wears a swaying garland
and who rides an elephant
about which people have to be warned
with beating drums—
is a just ruler.
Is he?
The bangles that slip off
my wrists
will themselves expose
the nature of his justice.

94

My mother keeps beating me
with a rod.
And the loveless neighbours
kill me with their words.
I suffer
on account of Valavan,
the powerful charioteer.
I am blamed for what I did not do,
just as the toad is blamed
for what it did not do
to the coconut.

95

While sulking
I turn my back to him.
While he hugs me
I bend my head shyly.
And while he makes love to me
I close my eyes
in ecstasy.
Could it be said
therefore
my eyes
haven't yet had their fill
of Valavan,
just ruler of the earth?

96

Young stork
with red legs,
let me touch your feet
in obeisance.
Do me a favour
when you reach Urandai in the south.
Tell the prince of the Kaveri land,
where fish leap and bound
and brush against the shore,
that I suffer for him.

97

When I was but a toddler,
my mother said,
'One day you will
marry the prince of Koli.'
What an irony!
I am now forbidden
even to look at him.
How the tables are turned!
Like a mirage in the wilderness
that deludes a thirsty animal.

98

Looking at the handsome shoulders
of Sembian who wears a swaying garland,
she became enamoured of him
even though I warned her.
Now, alas,
all her beauty is gone
and pallor has taken its place.
My words of warning useless,
like lighting a fire
on the surface of water.

99

Friend,
he was a young man
from the land of flowing waters,
where honeycombs hang
from coconut clusters.
It is true I met him
in my dream.
But alas,
I didn't make love to him.
My sulking
had gone too far.

100

My bashfulness
holds me back,
but love
melts my heart.
My eyes are hungry
for the sight of Killi
with his beautiful arms.
At this hour of midnight,
my heart rushes forward and backward
like an ant
caught between two fires.

101

My heart,
you are very brave.
Do not be coy
when he stands before you.
Paying homage to him—
this lord of bountiful rivers,
whose triumphant flag
has as its emblem the tiger—
you must fully reveal to him
the plight of my arms
and beg of him:
'Can't you show mercy
as a ruler?
Are your eyes made of wood?'

102

Biting winter wind:
are you the devil himself?
Are we poor females
your bonded serfs?
You have come to persecute us
even as Killi—
tamer of elephants,
master charioteer
and our protector—
is off his guard.

103

Caressing lotuses
and blue lilies
from the Chola land
of Nalankilli, the terrifying lancer,
a bee has arrived
as the king's messenger.
Keep off,
icy north wind,
the city is not like before—
it is well guarded now.

104

When I held the pestle
in my hands
I was determined
not to utter the name of Killi,
wearer of war anklets
and necklaces of gold.
How is it that
when I start pounding,
my heart and tongue
are filled with nothing
but the name of Killi,
the ruler of Koli,
that water-rich city?

105

Looking at his feet
I thought he was
the sea-coloured god.
But when my eyes reached
up towards his chest
he appeared to be
the god of the *konrai* garland.
Only when I looked at his head
and saw the *athi* flowers
did I become convinced
that he was the king Valavan.

106

The god of love
with his serrated bow
and the Chola king Killi,
ever victorious in wars,
differ in the colour of their skin.
For the love-god,
son of Thirumal,
is dark-skinned
whereas the son
of the Uraiyur king
is fair.

107

Young maidens
gazing at Killi,
of the huge, mountain-like shoulders,
riding a horse
worship the horse,
their eyes filling with tears.
But, trying to conceal their tears,
they attempt to provide a reason
for them—
they say
there's dust in their eyes.

THE CHERA PRINCE

THE CHURA PRINCE

His Glory

108

The earth is like the sky.
Just as the stars
are the rulers of the earth
and the moon is supreme
among the stars,
so is the Chera king Kothai
the lord of the sky-scraping Kolli hills.

109

The spear with which
Prince Kothai—
who wears a garland
of fresh-blown flowers—
killed his enemy kings
is sharp at both ends.
One end reeks of raw flesh
and the other
is fragrant with sweet sandal paste.
Therefore,
jackals mill around
one end of the spear
while on the other,
honeybees swarm.

110

The land of Kothai,
deft wielder of a spear
with poison-tipped, leaf-shaped head,
knows no turmoil
except that
caused by the water birds.
For when the red lilies
bloom in the waterlogged fields,
the birds panic,
thinking the water is on fire.
They fly helter-skelter,
trying to guard their nestlings
under their wings.

His City

111

The drunkards
offer liquor
to the inebriate
and they,
with trembling hands,
allow it to spill
and gather in pools.
When the passing elephants
trample on this,
the streets of the garden city
of Vanchi
turn muddy.

Tributes He Received

112

O kings,
you who possess armies of elephants,
pay your tributes now and live!
And fix the symbol of the bow
to the walls of your fortresses.
For even the gods survive
by having his symbol
fixed on their skies!

His War Elephants

113

Tearing to shreds
the large white canopies
of dauntless enemy kings,
the angry elephant of Kothai
is mad for more conquests.
He raises up his trunk
to reach for the moon.

His Battlefield

114

In the battlefield
where the enemies of Pooliyan
lie dead,
with their emerald bracelets
and diamond-studded wristbands,
young jackals
greedy for the flesh of the dead
bite at the bands and bracelets
that cut up their mouths.
They howl in pain
and call for help.

Ruining Enemy Lands

115

Fertile fields,
all burned
and charred to ashes,
grow rank with thorny bushes.
And jackals roam the plains in packs.
This is the plight of the countries
of the kings
who caused the eyes
of Kothai—
who routs his enemies
with his elephant forces—
to become bloodshot.

116

Trailing vines of wild gourd,
blooming spiderwisp and
deep-rooted crabgrass growing rank
hide the village from view.
This is the plight of
the land of the enemies
who provoked the anger
of the shining spear of Kothai,
king of Musiri,
who wears a garland
of unfurling buds.

His Infatuates Complain

117

Look at the doors in this street!
All have worn-out hinges.
For mothers keep shutting them
and daughters keep throwing them open.
This happens
whenever the prince Kothai,
wearing fresh flower garlands
and riding a sturdy horse,
passes along the street
and love-mad girls
rush to have a glimpse of him.

118

O prince of Mandai—
router of enemies,
whose broad chest
would shame a mountain
and who keeps
an army of lancers—
is it proper on your part
to rob bangled maidens
of their beauty
and invite such comments
from their mothers:
'This is no just ruler'?

119

Having had a glimpse
of Kothai riding
in his horse-drawn carriage
my body lost its healthy glow.
But what of it?
The sallowness that spreads
over my skin
is like a sprinkle of gold.
It is many hundred times
more precious
than what I have lost.

120

My heart is on fire
on account of Kothai,
the ruler of Pooli
and master of war-loving elephants.
O village folk!
Extinguish this fire,
and save me
with your mercy
which is like water and shade.

121

Indignant
that I should stare at
the prince Kothai,
owner of a fleet,
my mother
keeps the front door shut.
But will she also shut
the mouths of gossipmongers,
linking my name with his?

122

The ruler of Mandai—
a land surrounded by coconut groves,
laurel woods,
brimming lakes
and blossoming *naga* trees—
caressed my body
one dark night.
It was only in my dream.
But how is it that these girls
know about it?

123

To have a glimpse of
the prince Kothai,
who wears a necklace
of the choicest diamonds
and a swaying garland,
I rushed to the front door.
But I found myself
closing the door
instead of opening it.
And I stood there, torn between
desire and modesty,
like the needy poor
who tarry at a rich man's door,
torn between penury and dignity.

124

My lovelorn heart
went out of my body
to meet Kothai,
who wears swaying garlands
and necklaces of
the choicest gems.
Now in the harsh winter,
what has happened to my heart?
It must be standing
at the huge palace gates,
arms wrapped around its body
in the severe cold.

125

Poor lovelorn girl!
She was telling all her friends,
'Let the king of the western country,
who rules from Vanchi, come!
I'll rail at him!'
Her heart was mutinous.
But the moment she set
her eyes on him
all her rebelliousness vanished.

126

'He is the thief
who stole my beauty!'
'He is the thief
who broke into the sanctum of my heart!'
These are the accusations
hurled at Kothai, the Chera prince,
wherever he goes.

127

To cure me of my illness,
my mother bathed me
and took me to an altar
prepared by sprinkling
a black goat's blood.
But how can they cure me?
It is no illness.
It is passion
for the prince Kothai,
wielder of a deadly spear
and winner of many a battle.

128

Though Makadunkone,
ruler of Mandai—
land of flowing waters—
is great as a king,
we must make clear to him
our hearts' grievances.
The world is like that,
my friend
whose lovely forehead
is adorned
with a *pottu*.

129

The god who rides a bull
and the Chera king,
a war veteran,
are alike
in power and in authority.
But in one aspect
they differ.
The god of the deadly axe
has three eyes.
The king has but two.

130

He cannot be Indra
for he has just a pair of eyes.
Nor can he be
the god of heaven
who rides a bull,
for he wears no crescent on his head.
Can he be the god
with a rooster on his flag?
No, that too cannot be
for he has but one face.
So now we know:
he is none other than
Kothai, king of kings.

NOTES

Poem 1
> *Aathirai*: The sixth star in the traditional Indian calendar, considered to be the birth star of Siva.

Poem 2
> **the lord who rides a peacock:** Murugan, the ancient Tamil god.

Poem 4
> The feats of Thirumal (Vishnu) in his Krishna avatar are identified in this poem with those of the Pandya king. Krishna killed a demon who took the form of a horse.

> **pot-dance:** Krishna performed the pot-dance to free Aniruddha, the son of Kama, the love-god.

> **Punthodi:** Nappinnai, the cowherd girl, the beloved of Krishna in Tamil Vaishnava tradition.

Poem 7
> *Uthiradam*: The twenty-first lunar asterism in the traditional Indian calendar.

Poem 10
> **the celestial ones do not tread the earth:** It is believed that the feet of the devas do not touch the ground, nor do their eyes blink.

Poem 19

women from the enemy side immolating themselves: The custom of war widows burning themselves on their husbands' funeral pyre.

Poem 24

mounting his proud elephant: An ancient custom, *kudainatkol*, of parading the royal canopy on the elephant as a challenge to enemy kings or as a call to war.

Poem 31

play the game of *koodal*: *Koodal-ilaithal*, an ancient game. To test their luck, girls draw continuous looping rings on the sand with their fingers. The loops meeting together augur fulfilment of their wish. Koodal is also another name for Madurai. The term also suggests sexual union. The poet plays on these meanings of *koodal*.

Poem 34

with every stroke of the pestle: An ancient custom of women singing in praise of a hero when husking grain in a standing position with a mortar and pestle. This reference is also made in poem 104.

Poem 50

***thudi*:** A small double-sided drum.

Poem 59

Vanchi: As a verb, it refers to betrayal or desertion. As a noun, it refers to the capital city of the Cheras. The poet plays on both meanings: he will not betray, and he is no Chera king but a Pandya.

Poem 60

***ulundu*:** Black gram.

Poem 62

Mantara mountain: In Hindu mythology, the mountain used to churn the oceans by the gods and demons to yield a plethora of supernatural objects.

Poem 63

broke the *kurunda* tree; . . . dark mole on your chest: references to mythological stories in Krishna's life.

Poem 64

god of the basil garland: Thirumal.

obtained by begging: a reference to the myth where Vishnu in his Vamana avatar acquired the three worlds from king Mahabali as alms.

Poem 70

***thali*:** Wedding chain. It is ritually removed at the husband's death.

Poem 82

Only the spiders lose their webs: It is customary to spruce up homes and dust away the cobwebs on festive days.

Poem 84

to save the life of a fugitive pigeon: A legendary story about an ancient Chola king. To save a pigeon who sought his refuge, the king offered an equal amount of his own flesh to the pursuing hawk. Miraculously the scales wouldn't weigh down and the king proffered his whole body.

Poem 87

***kayal* fish:** The carp; a conventional, even clichéd, simile for the eyes of beautiful women.

Poem 88

> **my innocent arms are being punished**: In love-sickness the arms are said to become thin; a poetic motif.

Poem 92

> **heartless cruelty of the cowherd's flute**: The music of the flute is said to accentuate the pain of separation in love.

Poem 94

> **toad is blamed**: A popular belief that when a coconut, broken open, is found to be blighted, a toad is said to have eaten it away.

Poem 97

> **One day you will marry the prince**: Playful promises and hopes given to young children, especially regarding marriage.

Poem 102

> **Biting winter wind**: The winter wind, coming from the north, is said to heighten the pain of parting in love.

Poem 105

> **sea-coloured god**: Thirumal.

> **the lord of the *konrai* garland**: Siva.

> These references exhibit the poetic conceit of praising the Chola king as Thirumal and Siva.

Poem 112

> **the gods survive by having his symbol fixed on their skies**: Poetic conceit of referring to the rainbow as affixed by the gods to prevent an invasion by the Cheras, whose royal emblem is the bow.

Notes

Poem 127

sprinkling a black goat's blood: Mistaking the girl's lovesickness for a malady caused by the possession of a spirit, the girl's mother performs rituals to exorcise it.

Poem 129

The poet equates the king with Siva.

Poem 130

god of heaven who rides a bull: Siva.

god with a rooster on his flag: Murugan, the ancient Tamil god.

ACKNOWLEDGEMENTS

If a master translator who could not find a publisher for fifty years now has two published books in a reputed imprint, the credit in large measure should go to R. Sivapriya. Sivapriya enthusiastically endorsed my proposals to Penguin and provided excellent editorial support. Ambar Sahil Chatterjee was meticulous in his copyediting.

Y. Manikandan kindly permitted me to consult his forthcoming edition of *Muttollayiram* which has enriched this volume. Kesavan Veluthat commented on an earlier version of the introduction. Whitney Cox once again ran his fine pen over the manuscript and polished it. S. Thillainayagam helped with the proofs. My wife Anitha keyed-in the text during our honeymoon!

M.L. Thangappa and I fondly remember Tha. Kovendhan (1932–2004), his dear friend and my mentor, for bringing us together and for his undying faith in our abilities.

Thangappa and I dedicate this book to Visalakshi Thangappa and Anitha Chalapathy. What would we be without them?

Chennai   A.R. Venkatachalapathy
8 March 2011